Contents

D0530370

Let's Get Rolling

Wheels are amazing! From ancient racing **chariots** to modern motocross bikes, wheels make the world go round.

WILD WHEELS

Peter Millett

OXFORD
UNIVERSITY PRESS

OXFORD
UNIVERSITY PRESS

Great Clarendon Street, Oxford, OX2 6DP, United Kingdom

Oxford University Press is a department of the University
of Oxford. It furthers the University's objective of excellence
in research, scholarship, and education by publishing
worldwide. Oxford is a registered trade mark of Oxford
University Press in the UK and in certain other countries

British Library Cataloguing in Publication Data
Data available

ISBN: 978-0-19-830809-6

10 9 8 7 6 5

Paper used in the production of this book is a natural, recyclable product
made from wood grown in sustainable forests. The manufacturing process
conforms to the environmental regulations of the country of origin.

Printed in China by Golden Cup

Acknowledgements

Series Editor: Nikki Gamble
Cover photo: Brian Bailey/Getty Images, gst/Shutterstock

Illustrations by Alan Brown
Designed and typeset by Ana Cosma

The publishers would like to thank the following for the permission
to reproduce photographs: **p1**: Shutterstock/homydesign; **p2/3**: Getty
Images; **p4**: Niday Picture Library/Alamy; **p5**: Yuri Arcurs/istockphoto; **p6**:
Creative Crop/Getty Images; **p7**: AFP/Getty Images; **p8**: Getty Images; **p9**:
HomeArt/Shutterstock; **p10**: Chungking/Shutterstock; **p11**: Javier Larrea/
Age Fotostock; **p12**: MaxkateUSA/Shutterstock; **p13**: Richard Heathcote/
Getty Images; **p15t**: Back Page Images/REX; **p15b**: Andy Crawford/Getty
Images; **p16**: Sipa Press/REX; **p17b**: Creative Crop/Getty Images; **p17t**:
Radu Razvan/Shutterstock; **p18**: Margo Harrison/Shutterstock; **p19**: Mirco
Lazzari gp/Getty Images; **p20**: Transtock/Masterfile; **p21**: Michael Stokes/
Shutterstock; **Background images** by Nicemonkey/Shutterstock; Jamie
Farrant/istockphoto; Leontura/istockphoto; ElenaShow/Shutterstock; Miloje/
Shutterstock; RoyStudio.eu/Shutterstock; Eky Studio/Shutterstock; EugenP/
Shutterstock; **back cover**: gst/Shutterstock

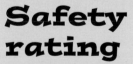

Safety rating

This book includes some wild tricks.
Don't try them at home — you have to be:

 an expert

⚠ ⚠ a professional stunt person

⚠ ⚠ ⚠ totally nuts!

Fun on Wheels

BMX BIKES

BMX bikes are for kids who love riding off-road. Their lightweight but strong frames and tyres with thick **tread** are perfect for doing jumps and zooming up hills.

Most BMX bikes have 36 **spokes** per wheel.

strong lightweight frame

tough tyres with thick tread

⚠ **Wild wheel tricks**

Footjam tailwhip

The rider spins the back of
the bike around in a circle.

SKATEBOARDS

Skateboards were invented by surfers in the 1950s. Today, around 50 million people ride them. Skateboarders do amazing tricks and stunts!

very light board

small plastic wheels

In 1978, 14-year-old Alan 'Ollie' Gelfand invented the stunt known as the 'ollie'.

⚠ **Wild wheel tricks**

Ollie

The rider launches into the air, staying on the board the whole time.

RAZOR SCOOTERS

Razor scooters were invented by a factory owner after he got tired of walking around his massive factory. Soon, everybody wanted one!

Scooters in the early 1900s had steel wheels. Kids loved the loud noise they made.

fold-down handlebars

small, tough and quiet plastic wheels

⚠ **Wild wheel tricks**

Tailwhip

The rider twirls the bottom of the scooter around in a circle.

Fast Wheels

INLINE SKATING

In 1979, Scott and Brennan Olson swapped the blades on their ice-hockey boots for wheels. The wheels were in one line, which made the skates go faster!

Early inline skates couldn't turn left or right – and they had no brakes. **Ouch!**

boot

brake

four plastic wheels

⚠️ ⚠️ Wild wheel tricks

Hand plant

The skater does a one-handed handstand while grabbing their skate.

WHEELCHAIR RACING

Racing wheelchairs have three wheels, just like tricycles – but they go a lot faster! The two back wheels are tilted towards the rider. This makes them easier to push.

In the UK's Tyne Tunnel race, wheelchair athletes reach almost 80 kilometres per hour. That's as fast as a lion can run!

⚠ ⚠ ⚠ Wild wheel tricks

Backflip

The wheelchair athlete does a backflip, using the ramp for speed.

large wheels

light frame

BICYCLE RACING

Road-racing bicycles are really light, with special spokes to help their wheels turn quickly. They are used for both **sprints** and long-distance races, like the Tour de France which lasts for three weeks.

⚠️ Wild wheel tip

Super-fast speeds

When going downhill, riders bend their knees and crouch low over their handlebars. They can reach speeds of 100 kilometres per hour!

Some racing bicycles have disc wheels instead of spokes. Discs create less **drag** than spokes when there is no wind.

drop-down handlebars

carbon spokes

Crazy Wheels

MOTOCROSS MADNESS

Motocross bikes are the toughest motorcycles ever made. They have very strong tyres that help the rider to race around corners and fly over bumps and jumps.

Arenacross is a mini version of motocross, held on dirt tracks in arenas and stadiums.

tough lightweight spokes

thick tread for extra grip

⚠️ ⚠️ ⚠️ Wild wheel tricks

Superman

The rider flies through the air, kicking their legs out behind the bike.

MONSTER TRUCKS

The first monster truck was made in 1981, when
Bob Chandler put huge wheels on his truck, 'Bigfoot'.
The wheels were taller than most children! Bob used
the giant wheels to crush cars and do amazing stunts.

Wild wheel tricks

Slap wheelie

After jumping over an object, the driver stands the monster truck on its back wheels.

John Seasock won the 2007 Monster Jam World Finals championship in 'Batman', a truck shaped like the Batmobile.

huge thick tyres

Wild Wheels

BMX bike

Number of wheels: 2

Estimated top speed:
50 kilometres
per hour

Skateboard

Number of wheels: 4

Estimated top speed:
16 kilometres
per hour

Razor scooter

Number of wheels: 2

Estimated top speed:
16 kilometres
per hour

Inline skates

Number of wheels:
8 (per pair)

Estimated top speed:
30 kilometres
per hour

Wrap-up

Racing wheelchair

Number of wheels: 3

Estimated top speed:
80 kilometres
per hour
downhill

Road-racing bicycle

Number of wheels: 2

Estimated top speed:
100 kilometres
per hour
downhill

Motocross bike

Number of wheels: 2

Estimated top speed:
110 kilometres
per hour

Monster truck

Number of wheels: 4

Estimated top speed:
110 kilometres
per hour

Glossary

BMX: a type of bicycle; BMX stands for 'bicycle motocross'

chariots: horse-drawn vehicles with two wheels

drag: when air pushes against an object, slowing it down

spokes: metal rods running from the middle of the wheel to the rim

sprints: fast races over a short distance

tread: the patterned, rubber part of a tyre that helps it grip the ground

Index